SHELLS
OF THE
FLORIDA COASTS

Drawings and Descriptions
by
FRANCIS WYLY HALL

A Great Outdoors Book

Great Outdoors Publishing Company
St. Petersburg, Florida

ISBN 0-8200-0207-0

Great Outdoors Publishing Company
4747 28th Street North
St. Petersburg, FL 33714

Printed in the United States of America

ABOUT THE BOOK

Great Outdoors has had a long and close relationship with Francis Wyly Hall, the author of this little book. We were Mrs. Hall's prime distributor since she first started publishing her popular little Florida books.

In the early 50's, I was on the road selling Great Outdoors' books as well as Mrs. Hall's titles. Her books were sold everywhere — from the Seminole Indian trading posts deep in the Everglades to every tourist stop along the ocean highway known as AIA. This was before the days of Waldens, B. Daltons, or other chain bookstores. Mrs. Hall was a pioneer writer-publisher at the same time Great Outdoors Publishing Company was founded. We were friendly competitors.

Several years ago, Mrs. Hall died and Great Outdoors bought her copyrights. Each of her titles is being revised and reissued. They are still the same popular Francis Wyly Hall books. We just added some new color pages, reset the type, and freshened up the shell drawings. We hope you enjoy this book as much as the thousands of other people who came to know this pioneer lady by way of the "Hall books."

Charlie Allyn,
Publisher,
GREAT OUTDOORS PUBLISHING CO.

SOME INFORMATION ABOUT
SHELLS AND MOLLUSKS

The study of shells is a very fascinating hobby for young and old alike, and there is no place in the world better suited to the gathering of specimens than some of our Florida beaches, especially those on the West Coast. Some of the best are: Sanibel, Pass-A-Grille, Marco Island, Treasure Island, Sarasota, Clearwater, Bonita Springs, Bradenton, Naples, Cape Romano, and Key West.

Shells range in size from those so tiny one can barely see them, to the Giant Clam which weighs five hundred pounds. Shells are found throughout the world except in the polar regions. Their colors include all the colors of the rainbow and they are often marked with beautiful symmetric patterns. They are lined with polished enamel or mother-of-pearl.

The animals that live inside these shells are as interesting as the shells themselves. They are called Mollusks. Some are brilliantly colored, and many of them are very active. Some are edible, such as the clams, oysters and scallops. They also provide food for fish, and act as scavengers along our beaches. They reproduce by laying eggs, each species having its own method of protecting the unhatched eggs. Some shells construct leathery capsules of various shapes, some secrete them in masses of gelatinous substance, some attach them to seaweed. The bivalves retain their eggs in the parent shells until hatched. A few bring forth their young alive.

Mollusks are divided into two principal classes — Univalve and Bivalve, of which about 75% are univalve. The univalve has a single shell, built on the spiral plan. The animal which inhabits this shell has a head bearing a long, flexible tongue which contains rows of sharp teeth. By means of this radula, the univalves, many of which are carnivorous, bore holes in other shells and devour the animals. Some univalves lack radula or have only isolated, long barb-like teeth (cones, auger shells, etc.).

Their chief prey are the bivalves, but they sometimes eat their own kind. The mollusk has a well-developed sense of smell and touch, but its sight and hearing are of a low order. The large, strong muscle which can be seen protruding from the aperture of the shell is called the foot. Attached to this is the perculum, or door, with which the mollusk shuts itself into its house. The outer shell in the live state is often covered with a protective skin, called the epidermis.

The bivalve mollusk has two shells, joined by a hinge. The animal is generally considered to be on a lower scale of development than the univalve. It has no head and rarely has eyes, although the scallop has a hundred or more around the edge of its mantle. The mollusk has two tubes, called siphons. A constant flow of water is drawn into one siphon and discharged through the other. From this flow of water the bivalve obtains its food. This mollusk, too, has a well-developed plow-like foot by means of which he often pulls his house into the soft sand for protection from his many enemies, including man, the univalve mollusk, fish, starfish and even the sea gull.

All mollusks have a protecting outer skin called the mantle, which envelops the creature like a bag and it is from the glands in this mantle that the calcareous shell is secreted or built up, enlarging the shell along its outer edge as the animal within requires more room.

Nearly all shells are occasionally found in a rare, pure white or albino form. These are not bleached or faded, but are naturally pure white.

○　○　○

The size of a shell, as given in this book, refers to the average adult shell. Nearly all can be found smaller or larger.

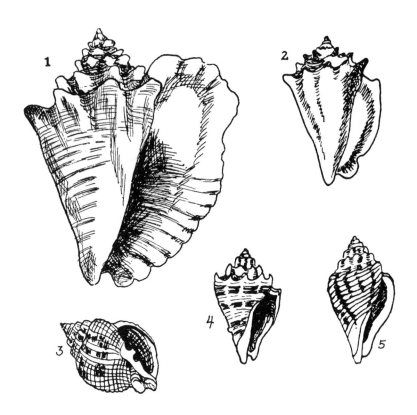

1. **Giant Conch** *(Strombus gigas).* Large, heavy shell; grows to 12 inches long; rough outside, with brown epidermis; inside polished, rich pink. Common in S. Fla. and Key West. Some people eat the flesh in Key West. Cameos are cut from the shells.

2. **Florida Fighting Conch** *(Strombus alatus).* Heavy, 3 to 4 inches long; outside tan or brown, with brown and white markings; lip polished, white, purple and orange. Common on west coast. The mollusk is very active and is carnivorous.

3. **Nutmeg** *(Cancellaria reticulata).* Heavy, rounded shell, 1 to 1½ inches long; white, banded and spotted with reddish brown; outside is deeply cut with cross-barred ridges; west coast. The animal is a vegetarian.

4. **King's Crown** *(Melongena corona).* A handsome shell of many varieties, found in bays on the west coast; 1 to 4 inches long, fine spiral ridges; colored with bands of dark brown or gray, and white; has a row of white spines around the shoulder, with sometimes a secondary row near the base; animal is aggressive and carnivorous.

5. **Baby Conch.** These are the young shells of the Fighting Conch, very common on the west coast; 1 inch long; cream with tan markings; fine spiral ridges, which are lost in the adult shells.

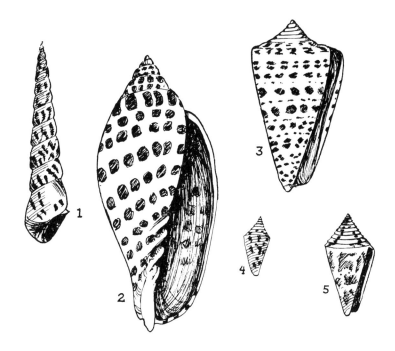

1. **Variegated Screw Shell** *(Turritella variegata)*. Long, slender shell, 5 inches long, with many whorls; comes to a very sharp point; mottled, dark brownish gray.

2. **Junonia** *(Scaphella junonia)*. A rare and majestic shell; creamy white, with rounded spots of reddish or brown; 3 to 4 inches long; lip thin, lined with white, the spots showing through faintly. This is a prized shell among collectors.

3. **Alphabet Cone** *(Conus spurius atlanticus)*. Smooth, heavy shell, 2 to 3 inches long; marked with rows of brownish or orange spots; aperature long and narrow; spire low. West coast. The animal preys on the bivalve mollusk. Cones, also, are prized among collectors, one of the species, *Conus gloria-maris,* is worth several hundred dollars.

4. **Jasper Cone** *(Conus jaspideus)*. A tiny, perfect cone, 1 inch long; small spiral ridges; mottled with brown; aperture and apex faintly tinged with lavender.

5. **Florida Cone** *(Conus floridanus)*. 1 to 1½ inches long; spire higher than that of *Conus proteus;* smooth, with irregular pattern of white and yellow, or light orange.

1. **Moon Shell** *(Natica canrena)*. Smooth, light brown shell, with spiral bands of white; bearing zigzag marks of chestnut; wide aperture is tinged with purple; carnivorous; 1 to 1½ inches.

2. **Four-Toothed Nerite** *(Nerita versicolor)*. Strong, spiral, rounded ribs; white checkered with black; 1 to 1½ inches across; small, white teeth are borne on columellar lip, feeds on seaweeds. Of the same family is Bleeding Tooth *(Nerita peloronta)*, whose teeth are splashed with reddish orange; outside tan, with reddish purple spots.

3. **Open Mouthed Purple** *(Thais patula)*. Very large aperture; short spire; spiral, knobbed ridges; dark brown and white.

4. **Spirula or Ram's Horn** *(Spirula spirula)*. Small, flat, loose, white spiral; shell is divided into chambers like that of the Nautilus.

5. **Baby's Ear** (*Sinum perspectivum*). East coast. Delicate, pure white, flattened shell, with snail-like spiral at one end; 1 to 1½ inches.

6. **West Indian Top Shell** *(Livona pica)*. When cleaned, has a pearly luster, greenish white, with wavy black markings; 4 inches high or less.

7. **Cat's Eye** *(Polinices duplicata)*. Tan or gray, smooth and polished aperture, lined with brown; found ½ to 3 inches in diameter. Naticas are carnivorous.

8. **Violet Snail** *(Janthina janthina)*. Fragile; lovely pale violet above, dark violet beneath; about 1 inch long.

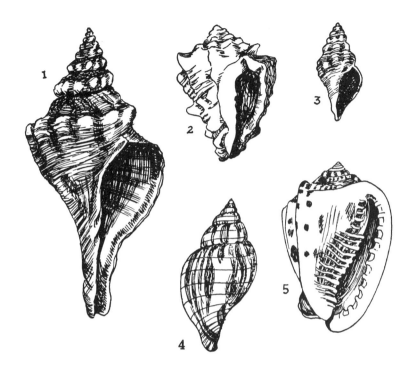

1. **Florida Horse Conch** *(Fasciolaria gigantea).* This is probably the largest of the univalve shells, 16 to 24 inches long; outer shell rough and horny, covered with dark epidermis; aperture is polished, deep, reddish orange. The animal is car..ivorous.

2. **Vase Shell** *(Vasum muricatum).* A very heavy shell; rough and worn-looking; lip slick; knobby points on the shoulder and 3 rows near the base; when cleaned, white, lined with pink; 3 to 5 inches; Fla. Keys.

3. **Baby Giant Band.** These little shells, 1 to 2 inches long, are found in yellow, orange or reddish.

4. **Banded Tulip** *(Fasciolaris hunteria).* Common in Florida waters. A graceful, smooth, rounded shell; gray, with chestnut or dark gray markings, and banded with black; hair lines; lip thin. Another variety is flesh-colored, with darker markings and the same hair lines. A dark red Tulip is found at Sanibel.

5. **Flame Helmet** *(Cassis flammea).* Large, heavy shell, decorated with shades of brown and tan in a wavy pattern; glossy, flesh-colored lip margins, marked with black spots; front of shell is 3-cornered; shoulder bears strong knobs. Two very similar shells are the King Helmet and the Queen Helmet. Carnivorous.

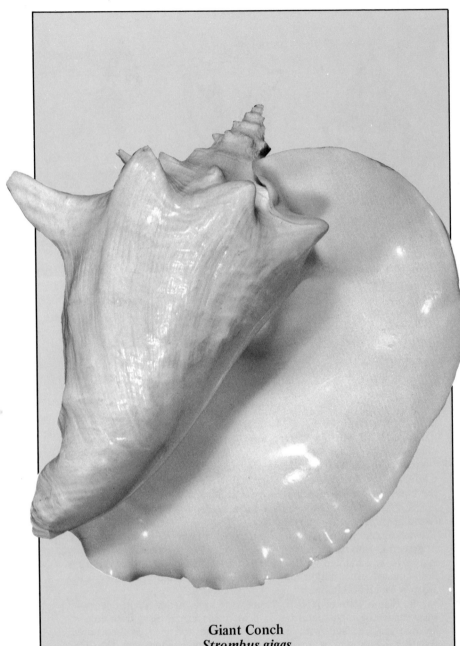

Giant Conch
Strombus gigas

Scotch Bonnets
Phalium granulatum

Apple Murex
Murex pomum

Lace Murex
Murex florifer dilectus

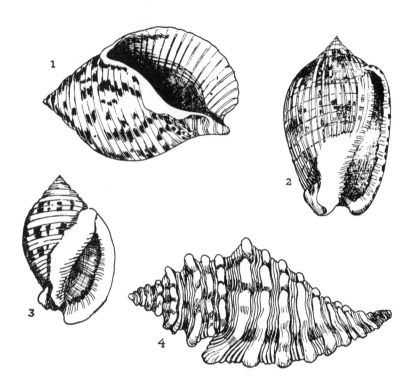

1. **Partridge Tun Shell** *(Tonna maculosa)*. Rather a thin shell, 5 to 8 inches long; light tan; flat ribs, painted with reddish-brown spots; aperture wide and flaring, polished brown.

2. **Reticulated Helmet Shell** *(Cassis testiculus)*. 3 to 4 inches long; low spire; longitudinal ribs, crossed by flat, low spiral ribs; tan, splotched with chestnut; lip and columella are polished, flesh-colored, toothed; lip is turned back, edged with black spots; animal carnivorous; Florida Keys, Key West.

3. **Scotch Bonnet** *(Phalium granulatum)*. 3 inches long; smooth, flat, spiral ribs; lip thickened and toothed; cream or bluish white, with square brown spots; aperture white; carnivorous; rather rare.

4. **Angular Triton** *(Cymatium femorale)*. South Florida and West Indies; 3 to 7 inches long; very heavy; brown; wide, raised revolving ridges, bearing angular knobs; between them are small ridges, reddish brown; knobs are yellowish; lip thick, lining polished. A genus of 150 or more species. The largest, 18 inches long, is the Triton's Trumpet, found in the Pacific islands.

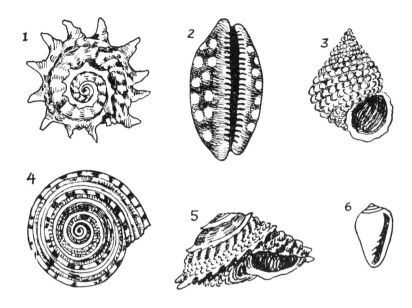

1. **Long-Spined Star Shell** *(Astraea longspina)*. A flattened cone, with a spiral row of spines around the outer edge; dirty white; pearly underneath; aperture pearly; base flat and sculptured; 1 inch high, 2 inches across.

2. **Measled Cowry** *(Cypraea zebra)*. A round, smooth, highly polished shell, dark brown on top, shading to bluish white beneath and bearing numerous round white spots. Underlying the outer brown color can be seen 3 bands of bluish brown.

3. **Beaded or Spiny Periwinkle** (*Tectarius muricatus*). A heavy little shell, 1 inch high; yellowish gray to brownish; spiral ribs, beaded with little knobs; Florida east coast.

4. **Granulated Sun Dial** *(Architectonica granulata)*. A flat shell, elaborately sculptured; surface has china-like quality; whorls violet, with upper edges white, spotted with brown; 2 inches across.

5. **Short-Spined Star Shell** *(Astraea brevispina)*. A cone 1½ inches high, 2 inches across the base; small spines along outer edge of whorls; dull white surface, marked by short ridges.

6. **Marginella** *(Marginella apicinum)*. Very abundantly found in Florida, 1/3-inch long; low spire; aperture nearly whole length of shell; highly glazed or polished; golden or white.

Nutmeg Shell
Cancellaria reticulata

Lion's Paw
Lyropecten nodosus

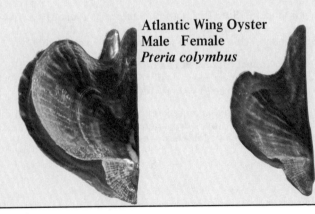

Atlantic Wing Oyster
Male   Female
Pteria colymbus

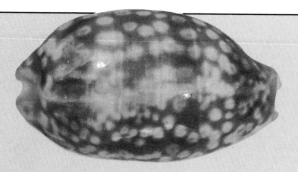

Measled Cowry
Cypraea zebra

Sunray Venus
Macrocallista nimbosa

Cat's Eye
Polinices duplicata

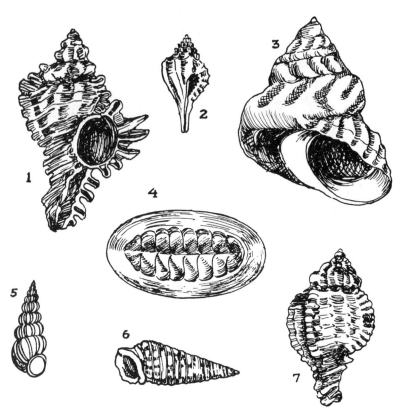

1. **Lace Murex** *(Murex dilectus).* Heavy; 3 inches long; most extravagantly sculptured, the spires and nodules resembling loops of lace; revolving ribs; white shading to reddish brown.

2. **Ribbed Oyster Drill** *(Eupleura caudata).* A curiously flattened little shell; 1 inch long; white, or shading to brown or pinkish.

3. **Green Star Shell** *(Astraea tuber).* Heavy, with diagonal wide ridges that follow down the whorls; ridges light, dark between; dirty white tinged with brown or green; aperture pearly.

4. **Coat-of-Mail** *(Chaetopleura apiculata).* Chitons in Florida waters are small and inconspicuous, found on dead shells or rocks; dark redbrown or gray; has 8 overlapping plates; curls up.

5. **Angulate Wentletrap** *(Epitonium angulata).* A pretty, small, white, spiral shell; 1 inch or less; well rounded whorls; high, white ribs.

6. **Florida Cerithium** *(Cerithium floridanum).* Strong, spiral ribs and circling rows of tiny nodules, giving a rough surface; 1 to 2 inches long; white and brown. Common on west coast.

7. **Apple Murex** *(Murex pomum).* Heavy; sculptured surface; spiral ribs; aperture large and round, with 3 brown spots on lip; yellow brown with brown spots; apex is pink; carnivorous.

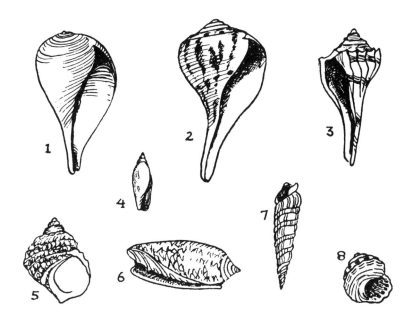

1. **Paper Fig** *(Ficus communis)*. Attractive, thin, delicate shell; 3 to 4 inches long; cream color; spiral ribs; wide aperture; polished brown lining; The mollusk is active and brightly colored.

2. **Pear Whelk** *(Busycon pyrum)*. 3 to 4 inches long; low spire; inconspicuous spiral ribs; white with yellowish or brown splotches. The whelks are carnivorous.

3. **Left-handed Whelk** *(Busycon perversum)*. Easily known by its lip being to the left. 3 to 5 inches long; pointed knobs around shoulder; tan with brown streaks. A dark whelk is found in bays. Very rarely a right-handed one is found.

4. **Rice Shell** *(Olivella floralia)*. A tiny, thin spiral shell, ½-inch long; translucent white, with wavy lines of brown. Florida east coast.

5. **Knobby Top** *(Turbo castaneus)*. Small, heavy shell with spiral beaded ridges; pearly underneath, covered with a thin layer of tan; round aperture is pearly.

6. **Lettered Olive** *(Oliva sayana)*. Both coasts. Heavy, smooth, polished; 1½ to 3 inches long; cream, marked with intricate lines of browns and grays.

7. **Dislocated Auger** *(Terebra dislocata)*. Slender spiral, 1 to 2 inches long; slate or brownish, with spiral bands of white, ridged and cross-ridged. Both coasts.

8. **Florida Button** *(Modulus modulus)*. West coast. Small, ½ inch to 1/3 inch across; low spire; ridges are noduled; white, gray, or tan.

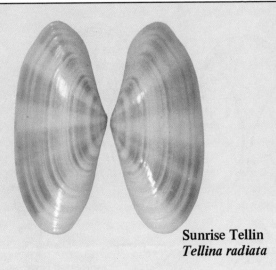

Sunrise Tellin
Tellina radiata

Disc Dosinia
Dosinia discus

Spotted Clam
Macrocallista maculata

Cat's Paw
Plicatula gibbosa

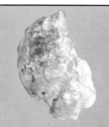

Coon Oyster
Lopha frons

Calico Scallop
Argopecten gibbus

Ornate Scallop
Chlamys ornata

Bay Scallop
*Argopecten irradians
concentricus*

Lettered Olive
Oliva sayana

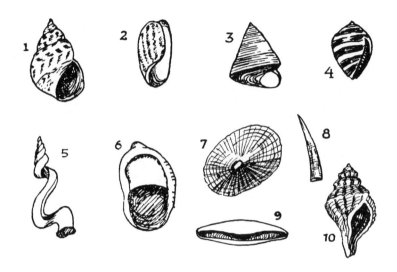

1. **Angulated Periwinkle** *(Littorina angulifera)*. Small, smooth shell, with chestnut dots in spiral lines, on brown or bluish-gray background.

2. **Florida Bubble** *(Bulla occidentalis)*. Thin, delicate, smooth shell; tan or gray with brown markings; 1 inch or less in length.

3. **Florida Top Shell** *(Calliostoma jujubinum perspectivum)*. ¾-inch high; brown; has fine spiral ribs, set with tiny white beads; base flat.

4. **Coffee Shell** *(Melampus coffeus)*. ½ inch long; dark brown or brownish gray and white bands.

5. **Worm Shell or Old Maid's Curl** *(Vermicularia spirata)*. Tan, gray or white.

6. **Boat Shell or Baby's Cradle** *(Crepidula fornicata)*. White or tan, with dark markings; lining brown; inside has thin shelf at one end. Similar is the White Slipper Limpet; flat, pure white; 1 inch long.

7. **Keyhole Limpet or Chinese Hat** *(Diadora alternata)*. Small, tent-shaped; small hole in top; ribbed; gray, tan or white with dark markings.

8. **Panelled Tooth Shell** *(Dentalium laqueatum)*. 9 to 12 prominent ribs; white; 1 inch long. Burrows into sand.

9. **Pointed Egg Shell** *(Simnia acicularis)*. Very smooth; thin; yellowish, is found on yellow seaweed.

10. **Florida Drill** *(Urosalpinx tampaensis)*. 1 inch long; yellowish or gray; sharp ribs; Florida west coast; lives on oysters.

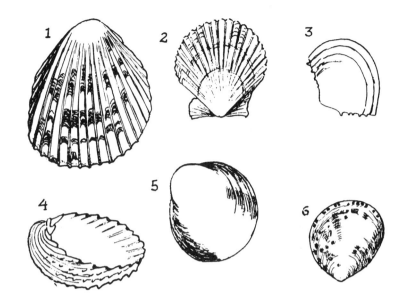

1. **Large or Brown Cockle** *(Cardium robustum).* A very fine shell, large and roomy; flat, deep ribs; yellowish-brown, marked with darker browns; inside is polished, rich brown; 3 to 5 inches in diameter.

2. **Many-Ribbed Scallop** *(Pecten irradians).* The common Scallop has well-marked ridges; scalloped edge; white, brown, yellow, orange, red, or gray; often one color rayed with another; diameter 1 to 2½ inches. The *Pecten gibbus* (versi-color) is white, mottled with purple or brownish.

3. **Crested Tellin** *(Tellidora cristata).* ¾ to 1 inch across; delicate; china-white; very flat, 3 lines around edge.

4. **Rose Cockle** *(Cardium isocardia).* Heavy; deep, notched ridges ending in point; yellowish with brownish purple markings; inside polished, rose or salmon, shading to purple; 2 inches across.

      Yellow Cockle *(Cardium muricatum).* Similar to above; lined with yellow; ridges not so rough.

5. **Egg Cockle** *(Laevicardium laevigatum).* Thin, polished shell, smooth; globose; creamy, tinged with golden; inside splotched with reddish brown; 1 to 2 inches high.

6. **Little Egg or Morton's Cockle** *(Laevicardium mortoni).* Pretty, smooth, polished little shell; fawn color with brownish markings; inside yellow splotched with reddish or purple, and a purple blotch near the hinge; often found double.

Tulip Horse Mussel
Modiolus americana

Ponderous Ark
Noetia ponderosa

Noah's Ark
Arca imbricata

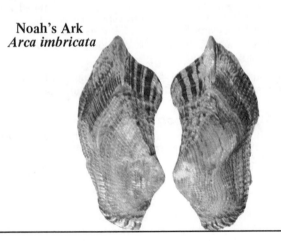

Tiger Lucina
Codakia orbicularis

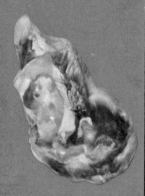

Eastern Oyster
Crassotrea virginica

Southern Quahog
Mercenaria campechiensis

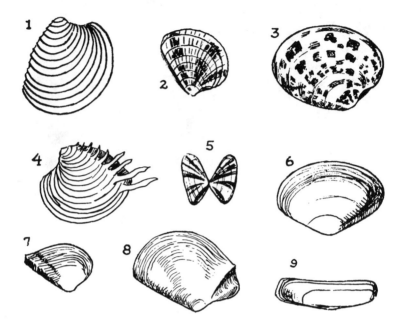

1. **Quahog or Hard-shelled Clam** *(Mercenaria mercenaria)*. Gray or white; thick shell with circular ridges; grows very large.

2. **Cross-barred Venus** *(Chione cancellata)*. Common; heavy; cross-ribbed; white with brown rays; purple, brown or orange lining; 1 inch across.

3. **Spotted Clam** *(Macrocallista maculata)*. Smooth; polished; tan; brown spots, lining white tinged with violet; 1 to 2 inches across. A very pretty shell.

4. **Royal Comb or Elegant Venus** *(Hysteroconcha dione)*. Heavy; white, scored with growth lines; brown epidermis; 4 inches long; young shells, thin and yellowish.

5. **Coquina** *(Donax variabilis)*. Smooth; polished; all colors, patterned in plaids or stripes; colored lining; ½ to 1 inch long.

6. **Solid Surf Clam** *(Spisula solidissima)*. Heavy; white, scored with growth lines; brown epidermis; 4 inches long; young shells, thin and yellowish.

7. **Pointed Venus or Thick-shelled Heart** *(Anomalocardia cuneimeris)*. ½ inch long; finely ridged; brownish tinged with violet; lining, light brown.

8. **Frail Clam** *(Mactra fragilis)*. Very thin; fragile; swollen; depressed at one end, with a sharp ridge; white; 2 inches long.

9. **Green Razor Clam** *(Solen viridis)*. Very thin, sharp-edged; greenish or violet, with olive epidermis; 2 inches long.

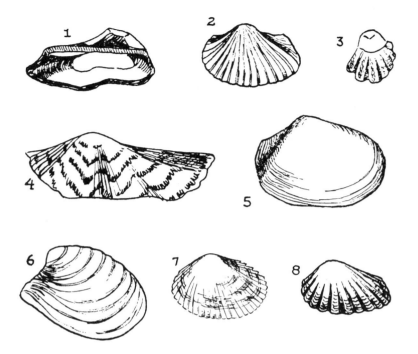

1. **Noah's Ark or Beaked Ark** *(Arca imbricata)*. Thick; worn and warped in appearance; brown; 2 to 3 inches long; lining lavender or white edged with brown.

2. **Transverse Ark** *(Anadara transversa)*. Box-shaped; ridged; pure white; found in quantities. Of the same family is . . .

   Ponderous Ark *(Noetia ponderosa)*. Short and thick; strong ribs; always has furry, black epidermis; 2½ inches long.

3. **Cat's Paw** *(Plicatula gibbosa)*. A flattened, irregular shell; plaited; surface is marked with rusty hair lines; ½ to ¾ inches long.

4. **Turkey Wing** *(Arca zebra)*. A heavy, strongly-ribbed shell; white with 'V'-shaped brown markings; lining white, edged with brown or tinged with violet; 2 to 4½ inches long.

5. **Atlantic Grooved Macoma or Saddle Shell** *(Apolymetis intastriata)*. Thin, but strong, pure white; 2 to 3 inches long; shell is bent at one end.

6. **Channelled Duck Clam** *(Labiosa plicatella)*. White; fragile; deeply grooved with smooth concentric ridges; has swollen appearance; fairly common; 2 to 2½ inches long.

7. **Spiny Paper Cockle** *(Papyridea soleniformis)*. Delicate, finely ribbed; pink, orange or lavender; brightly colored, polished lining; 1 inch long.

8. **Broad-ribbed Cardita** *(Cardita floridana)*. Strongly ribbed; 1 inch long; ribs reddish brown, darker toward edge, sometimes spotted.

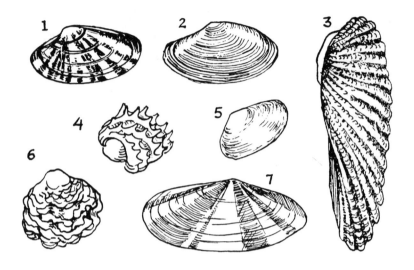

1. **Sunray Venus** *(Macrocallista nimbosa)*. Smooth and polished, with a plaid pattern of violet-gray or brown on a lighter background; lining white or shaded with orange; reaches length of 5 to 6 inches; often found double.

2. **Alternate Tellen** *(Tellina alternata)*. Translucent white shell; with fine concentric lines; 2 to 3 inches long; lining pink or yellow.

3. **Angel Wing** *(Cyrtopleura costata)*. Lovely; thin, delicate, pure white; much like an angel's wing in form, sculpture and color; 7 to 8 inches long. A much smaller variety is the False Angel Wing *(Barnea truncata)*.

4. **Chest Rock Oyster** *(Echinochama arcinella)*. Heavy; white; rows of spines on both valves; tinged with pink or orange; 1 to 1½ inches; weak hinge.

5. **Lined or Little Pink Tellen** *(Tellina lineata)*. Small and thin; ¾-inch long; lined with pinkish orange, which shows through from back; often found double.

6. **Leafy Jewel Box** *(Chama macerophylla)*. Bright yellow, pink or violet; both valves bear ruffles or fronds, the edges crimped; 1 to 2½ inches. Good specimens are rather rare.

7. **Sunrise Tellin** *(Tellina radiata)*. A beautiful shell with white, highly polished valves, painted with broad rays of deep pink; the inside also shows the rays, and is tinged with yellow; 2 to 3 inches long.

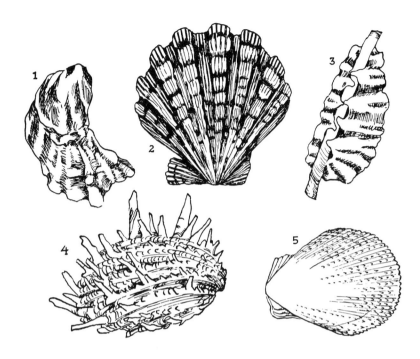

1. **Crested Oyster** *(Ostrea equestris)*. An irregular, misshapen, wavy shell; gray or brownish gray; 1½ to 2½ inches long.

2. **Lion's Paw** *(Lyropecten nodosus)*. A fine, showy shell; ranging in color from browns and purples to reds and oranges; 2 to 5 inches across; large ribs and set with blunt knobs.

3. **Bush Oyster** *(Ostrea spreta d'Orbigny)*. A queer-looking shell, brownish or gray, which develops small prongs to hold itself in place on a twig or branch.

4. **American Thorny Oyster** *(Spondylus americanus)*. In general, scallop-shaped, but irregular; white, shaded with pink, red, or yellow; young shells bear spines, as much as 3 inches long; the spines are shorter in the larger shells, and vary greatly in size and shape; shell itself is 3 to 6 inches long. A lovely shell.

5. **Rough Lima or Flat File Shell** *(Lima scabra)*. A shell of alabaster whiteness; 2 to 2½ inches long; set with rows of small file-like teeth.

The average shell collector must buy such shells as the American Thorny Oyster or the Lion's Paw, as they are found by dredgers or divers.

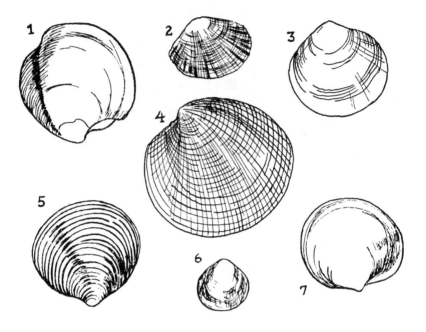

1. **Pennsylvania Lucina** *(Lucina pennsylvanica).* Heavy; alabaster white; straw-colored epidermis; has deeply-depressed diagonal furrow at the posterior end. Of the same family is Florida Lucine *(Lucina floridana),* white; smaller than *pennsylvanica* and with only an indication of the furrow.

2. **Cancellate Semele** *(Semele bellastriata).* ½ to ¾ inch long; inside polished, deeply colored; outside ridged, rays of reddish, purplish, or yellowish brown; often found in pairs, or alive.

3. **White Atlantic Semele** *(Semele proficua).* Nearly white, sometimes pinkish; plentiful; scored with fine growth lines outside.

4. **Tiger Lucine** *(Codakia orbicularis).* White, tinged with rose pink on edges; 3 inches across; outside bears fine cross ridges.

5. **Elegant Dosinia** *(Dosinia elegans).* White; polished; finely ribbed with concentric lines; 1 to 3 inches across; often found in pairs; yellowish brown epidermis.

6. **Atlantic Nut Clam** *(Nucula proxima).* Actual size; reddish brown.

7. **Buttercup Lucine** *(Anodontia alba).* Plentiful; white, bowl-shaped shell, with butter-colored lining, which sometimes shows through from back; scored with fine lines; 1¾ to 2½ inches across.

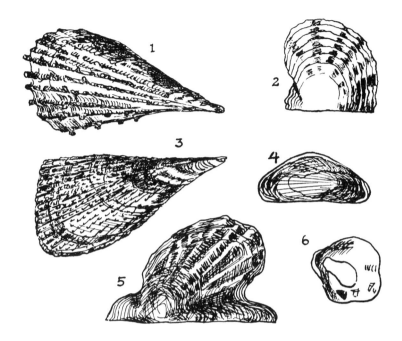

1. **Rigid Pen Shell** *(Atrina rigida).* Dark grayish, translucent shell; triangular wedge-shaped; very sharp edges; outer shell spiny; inside darkly iridescent, greens, blues and purples; 6 to 10 inches.

2. **Pearly Oyster** *(Pinctada radiata).* Thin, flat wing shells; outside drab and scaly; fringed edges; irregularly marked with brownish rays; inside mother-of-pearl, iridescent golds, greens & blues; 1½ to 2 inches.

3. **Fan or Half-naked Pen Shell** *(Atrina semi-nuda).* A thin, smoke-colored, almost transparent shell; outer surface set with sharp, raised scales in radiating rows; inside iridescent. These shells make a byssus, by which they attach themselves to rocks. This "golden fleece" can be spun and woven into fabric softer than any silk, from which gloves, scarves, etc., are made.

4. **Tulip Horse Mussel** *(Modiolus americana).* Thin; dark brownish gray; lined with iridescent purples; often held in clusters by the black thread-like byssus.

5. **Atlantic Wing Oyster** *(Pteria columbus).* Drab, reddish-brown; long, slender points or wings; valves rounded; edges soft; 3 to 4 inches long; lined with iridescent mother-of-pearl.

6. **Jingle Shell** *(Anomia simplex).* Thin and shiny; irregular; flat or cupped, print of baby's foot inside; yellow, orange, gray, black or translucent. Also called Baby's Foot or Chinese Money.

HOW TO CLEAN YOUR SHELLS

Most shells need only a little rubbing or brushing — but if necessary, shells may be cleaned by dipping them in a weak solution of muriatic acid and water, being careful not to get any on the hands. Do not leave the shells in the acid too long, as it sometimes eats the epidermis, or skin. White shells may be bleached by dipping them in a solution of Clorox and water. Live shells should be boiled for a few minutes, and the animals removed. The shell can be soaked in alcohol to help remove any odor.

Any coloring of your shells will be improved by rubbing a few drops of olive oil into them. Never leave them exposed to bright sunlight, as the colors will fade.

HOW TO MAKE A SHELL COLLECTION

In making a shell collection, choose a heavy cardboard. Sea green, gray, or dull tan are good colors. Glue the shells on with colorless liquid cement (obtainable at drug stores and dime stores). For heavy shells, a ring of pipe cleaner glued to the underside of the shell and then to the cardboard will hold them in place. Be sure to give them plenty of time to dry. Each shell may be named or numbered. It is convenient to cut the cardboard to fit a flat box, about 11 x 14 inches, or larger. It is best to group all of one kind together, and to put the bi-valves on one sheet of cardboard and the uni-valves on another. The sheets of cardboard can then be fitted into the box and safely carried.

INDEX

Latin Names

*Color pages denoted by
Italic type.*

Color pages denoted by italics.